D0793650

JAN 28 1991

GO FOR IT! ™

SWIMMING

FOR BOYS AND GIRLS

START RIGHT AND SWIM WELL

by Bill Gutman

with Illustrations
by Ben Brown

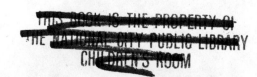
THIS BOOK IS THE PROPERTY OF
THE NATIONAL CITY PUBLIC LIBRARY
CHILDREN'S ROOM

MARSHALL CAVENDISH
CORPORATION

GREY CASTLE PRESS

Marshall Cavendish Edition, Freeport, New York.

No part of this publication may be reproduced in whole or in part, or stored in a retrieval system, or transmitted in any form or by any means, electronic, mechanical, photocopying, recording, or otherwise, without written permission of Grey Castle Press.

Published by arrangement with Grey Castle Press, Lakeville, Ct.

Copyright © 1990 by Grey Castle Press.

The *GO FOR IT* Sports Series is a trademark of Grey Castle Press.

Printed in the USA

The Library of Congress Cataloging in Publication Data

Gutman, Bill.
    Swimming : start right and play well / by Bill Gutman ; with
illustrations by Ben Brown.
        p.   cm. — (Go for it!)
    "Published by arrangement with Grey Castle Press, Lakeville, Ct."—
T.p. verso.
    Summary: Describes the history and competitive events of swimming
and provides instructions in the various strokes and methods.
    ISBN 0-942545-89-3 (lib. bdg.)
    1. Swimming—Juvenile literature. [1. Swimming.] I. Brown,
Ben, 1921–   Ill. II. Title. III. Series: Gutman, Bill. Go for
it!
GV837.6.G88   1990
797.2'1—dc20

89-7380
CIP
AC

Photo credits: Bettmann, page 8; Culver Pictures, page 10; Duomo/David Madison, page 9; Reuters/Bettmann, page 11; UPI, page 7.

Special thanks to: Connie Zaenglein, varsity swimming coach, Arlington High School, LaGrangeville, N.Y.

Picture research: Omni Photo Communications, Inc.

ABOUT THE AUTHOR

Bill Gutman is the author of over 70 books for children and young adults. The majority of his titles have dealt with sports, in both fiction and non-fiction, including "how-to" books. His name is well-known to librarians who make it their business to be informed about books of special interest to boys and reluctant readers. He lives in Poughquag, New York.

ABOUT THE ILLUSTRATOR

Ben Brown's experience ranges from cartoonist to gallery painter. He is a graduate of the High School of Music & Art in New York City and the University of Iowa Art School. He has been a member of the National Academy of Design and the Art Students' League. He has illustrated government training manuals for the disadvantaged (using sports as themes), and his animation work for the American Bible Society won two blue ribbons from the American Film Festival. He lives in Great Barrington, Massachusetts.

In order to keep the instructions in this book as simple as possible, the author has chosen in most cases to use "he" to signify both boys and girls.

A BRIEF HISTORY

There is really no way to tell when man first began to swim. It may have been purely the result of an accident, or it may have been a matter of survival. But it certainly wasn't for pleasure or competition.

In fact, man is not a natural swimmer. It is thought that the first men to try to move themselves through the water probably did so after watching animals swim. There are many drawings from ancient cultures showing people swimming in the water. The Egyptians, Greeks and Romans all swam and some of the strokes they used seem much like the strokes used today.

Swimming more or less declined in Europe during the Middle Ages, when people thought that water was a source of disease. During the early part of the 19th century, swimming became popular once more. People saw the activity as a new sport, where two or more swimmers could race against one another.

The Japanese organized swimming in the early part of the 17th century. It was part of their educational program. Because the country was more or less closed to the rest of the world until 1867, swimming did not spread from the Land of the Rising Sun.

There were six swimming pools opened in London, England, by around 1840. It was from about that point that swimming began to grow as an organized sport. Englishmen in Australia may have held the first international competition in Melbourne in 1858. Competitive swimming was also beginning to flourish.

By 1869, the London Sporting Association in England included swimming in its programs. Five years later, in 1874, the first national swimming federation was formed in England. A year after that, Captain Mathew Webb became the first man to swim across the English Channel. Much of competitive swimming in the early years was long-distance swimming.

The United States was not very far behind great Britain. Competitive swimming in the U.S. became organized with the founding of the Amateur Athletic Union in 1888. A year later, the first European championships were held in Vienna, Austria. However, it was really the growth of the Olympic Games that helped swimming to become the great sport it is today.

The modern Olympics were begun in Athens, Greece, in 1896, and swimming has always been a major part of the Olympic schedule. At the beginning, however, there were not nearly as many different races as there are today.

The breaststroke was the only racing stroke used during those first Games. The breaststroke was not a specialized stroke then, but was used in freestyle swimming. It wasn't long after, however, that swimmers began discovering other ways to swim faster.

First came the sidestroke, with the swimmer lying on his side in the water and using a scissors type of kick. Before long, some swimmers were lifting one arm out of the water completely. They were making a full, 180 degree arm stroke and found they went even faster. Then, in the late 1800s, an Englishman named John Trudgen came up with yet another new stroke.

Trudgen had been visiting South America and had seen the natives there swimming with a two-arm alternating stroke. The swimmer was on his belly in the water and using both arms in the 180 degree swing. But Trudgen still used the scissors kick. Then, in 1902, an Australian named Richard Cavill set a new record by swimming 100 yards in 58.6 seconds.

Donna De Varona won a pair of gold medals for the United States in the 1964 Olympics. Today she is a sports commentator on television.

Mark Spitz proved that practice makes perfect. Swimming for the United States in the 1972 Olympics, Spitz set a record by winning seven gold medals.

Matt Biondi was another United States swimming superstar. In the 1988 Olympics, he took seven medals, including five golds. In the process, he set four new world records.

The big news wasn't the time, but the fact that Cavill had made a change in Trudgen's stroke. Instead of a scissors kick, he used an up-and-down flutter kick. This became known as the Australian Crawl and is the basic freestyle racing stroke used today.

By 1912, women were also swimming in Olympic competition, and slowly but surely, the number of strokes and events grew. Today, the Olympics hold 13 swimming events for men and 13 for women. These same events are usually offered at most competitive meets.

Johnny Weissmuller was already starting his movie career when this picture was taken in 1932. With Weissmuller (left), were two members of the 1932 United States Olympic swim team. They are Clarence "Buster" Crabbe (center) and Al Swartz. Crabbe would become a gold medal winner and then follow Weissmuller to a career in the movies and television.

Janet Evans, at age 17, won three gold medals in the 1988 Olympics, including this one in the 400-meter individual medley. She proved once again that teenage swimmers are capable of being among the world's best.

Men's events include the 100, 200, 400 and 1,500-meter free-style events; the 100 and 200-meter backstroke; the 100 and 200 meter breaststroke, as well as 100 and 200 meter butterfly stroke. There are also three relay events. The 400-meter individual medley has one person swimming all four strokes. Then there is the 4 x 200-meter freestyle relay and 4 x 100-meter medley relay.

Women's events are almost the same. Instead of the 1,500-meter freestyle, women swim the 800-meter freestyle. In place of the 4 x 200-meter freestyle relay, women have the 4 x 100-meter freestyle relay. Otherwise, the events are identical.

The United States has dominated world swimming during many portions of the 20th century. But the Australians, Japanese and Germans have had strong teams and some outstanding individuals.

One of the great early freestyle swimmers was a Hawaiian named Duke Kahanamoku. The Duke never had a formal swimming lesson, yet he won the 100-meter freestyle at the Stockholm Olympics in 1912 and repeated his triumph at Antwerp eight years later.

Following in the Duke's wake was one of America's most famous swimmers, Johnny Weissmuller. He won three Olympic golds, two in Paris in 1924 and another in Amsterdam in 1928. Weissmuller's fame came not only from being a great swimmer, but also from his movie career, as the best known Tarzan of all time. His Tarzan movies can still be seen on television today.

Another American swimming champion to go on to a long movie and television career was Clarence "Buster" Crabbe, who won his gold in the 400-meter freestyle in 1932.

Other great American champions of recent vintage include Don Schollander, John Naber, Donna De Varona, Debbie Meyer and Mark Spitz. Spitz became a record-breaking legend in the 1972 Olympics, when he won seven gold medals, taking four individual and three more in the relays.

In the 1988 Olympics, the Americans again dominated the swimming events, this time led by Matt Biondi and Janet Evans. Biondi took seven medals—five gold, a silver and a bronze. Along the way, he set four world records. Evans, barely 17 years old, won three gold medals at the Olympics and has set a slew of world records in her short swimming career.

Swimming has come a long way since the days of the side-stroke. New training methods and great athletes have made records fall almost every year. Because swimmers become world class at an early age, there are new stars and new heroes almost every day.

ORGANIZED SWIMMING

There is perhaps no more popular sport in the United States than swimming. Most swimming, however, is the recreational kind, for fun. There is no racing, no winner and no loser. But millions of people are swimming, and in swimming, they are involved in one of the healthiest activities there is.

Except for the old, out-of-the-way swimming hole, most swimming activities are closely supervised. Whether it be a lake, beach, pool or other designated swimming area, there is always a trained lifeguard on hand. Everyone should learn to swim as soon as possible. It isn't difficult to find an organized program that teaches the fundamentals of swimming and water safety.

Since swimming is strictly an amateur sport, the governing body is still the Amateur Athletic Union (AAU). There are no professional swimming leagues or professional swimming meets. Nevertheless, swimming is a very well organized sport.

The United States Swimming Program, which was once a part of the AAU, has set up age-group swim competitions all over the country. They work with other organizations, such as the YMCA, and offer their program to various summer leagues and recreation programs. There are also vigorous swim programs in most high schools and colleges, and young people who want to race against others can do so under top-notch supervision.

Because of this strong base, there are also good coaches available at YMCAs, in parks, at beaches and, of course, in most schools. There are also American Red Cross safety and swim instructors who are trained in the latest rescue and lifesaving techniques. This makes the sport a very safe one for young people.

While swimming is not a professional sport, it is nevertheless well organized and extremely popular. The success of the United States Olympic Swim team every four years is proof that the program is working.

The Sport Of Swimming

Swimming is an extremely healthy activity. Nearly every muscle in the body is exercised as a person moves through the water. The sport also builds confidence and helps develop both strength and coordination. Practiced regularly, it can keep anyone physically fit.

Like running, there are a number of different ways to pursue swimming. One is simply recreational, a few hours frolicking in the pool or at the beach. Even that is good for you. But if you want to swim competitively, there is quite a variety of events from which to choose.

There are shorter events, much like the sprints at track and field meets. They take great bursts of strength and power. A swimmer in these short events, such as a 50 or 100-meter swim, will exert all his energy trying for every split second of speed he can get.

Longer events are like distance running. They take pacing and endurance. A swimmer who burns himself out early in the race won't have enough left to finish strong.

Then there are specialties. Like hurdlers and jumpers on the track team, there are swimmers who only swim the breaststroke, butterfly or backstroke. There is something for everyone.

Of course, for those who just want swimming to be a challenge, there is long distance, something like running the marathon in a track meet. It can be a special challenge, such as swimming the English Channel. Or perhaps trying to swim

As a rule, swimming is an easy sport to learn. It just comes naturally to some people. The most important thing is not to fear the water. That's why many infants have learned to swim before they learn to walk. They just don't fear the water and look at swimming as a happy, pleasurable activity.

around Manhattan Island. Distance swimmers, like distance runners, are always finding new worlds to conquer.

Competitive swimming aside, it is important for every person, young and old, to be able to swim, to handle himself in the water. If a person does not fear the water, learning to swim can be easy and fun. The fact is that many infants have been taught to swim long before they could walk. The reason is that they have no fear of the water.

Step one is learning to swim. Then you can decide whether you might want to become a competitive swimmer. As with other sports, becoming competitive has its demands. It means having a good coach to teach the proper techniques. Then there is training. It must be done regularly with the swimmer following his coach's directions to the letter.

There must also be sacrifices. As part of a team, a swimmer must keep himself in condition, eat the proper foods and get plenty of rest. By doing this, he will not only benefit himself, but also his teammates. He must learn all about his sport and decide, along with his coach, which events are best suited for him. Finally, he must work hard to be the best swimmer he can be.

To some, throwing a buddy into a pool or lake is great fun. But this kind of prank can be very dangerous. The person being thrown in can strike his head on the end of the pool or dock. Or he might land on someone below, injuring both. Rule number one— don't horse around when the water is involved.

Basic Water Safety

Whether a person is a beginning swimmer or someone who has been swimming for years, he must still practice safe habits in and around the water. Everyone who swims must be ready to handle emergency situations. The best way to do this is to never panic. No matter what the crisis, try to remain calm.

The first thing that all swimmers should know is to never swim alone. Remember the old buddy system? It really works. If you want to practice or train, or just go for a fun swim, always have someone with you. Chances are you'll be swimming in water over your head, and accidents can happen. Having a second person along could save your life.

A pool is a fairly safe place because it is a known body of water. Everyone can tell the deep end from the shallow end. Still, that's no reason to horse around. Don't ever jump in without looking to see if someone is below, and never throw someone else in as a joke. Many a joke has resulted in a serious injury because someone has hit his head on the side of the pool. A good lifeguard will usually stop the nonsense before it starts.

However, a great deal of swimming around the country is not done in pools. People swim in lakes, streams, rivers, old fashioned swimming holes and even the ocean. It's important for all swimmers to know the water conditions where they are swimming. Before you jump or dive, know how deep the water is. Also try to find out what kind of bottom is down there. A glass or metal cut can be painful and dangerous.

In a river or stream, try to know the currents. A strong current can be a tough match for even the best swimmers. Don't ever swim out too far, away from the others, where people can't see you or reach you very quickly. And don't make the mistake of thinking you're better than you really are.

Muscle cramps while swimming can be annoying, painful and sometimes dangerous. If you get a foot or leg cramp while swimming, relax and float on your back. Then reach down and try to massage the area of the cramp. When the cramp goes away, try to resume swimming with a different stroke so the same muscle won't cramp again.

Swimmers who stay in too long or train too hard sometimes get painful muscle cramps. These, too, can be dangerous, especially if the swimmer panics. A swimmer with a foot or leg cramp should relax and immediately assume a floating position on his or her back. Then he should bring the cramped leg close to the surface of the water. He can now reach down and begin rubbing the muscle with both hands.

It's best to alternate the rubbing with a kneading or pinching action. Don't be gentle. Really work the cramped muscle to try to loosen it up. Sometimes even a brisk slapping action will help stop the muscle from cramping. When you're ready to swim on, try to use a different stroke from the one you used when you got the cramp. Other muscle groups will be used, and the cramp is less likely to come back. Always move slowly, but smoothly, and head to shore immediately.

A stomach cramp can be even more dangerous. This is usually caused by swimming strenuously in cold water on a full stomach. Pain from a stomach cramp can be very sharp and cause a swimmer to double over in the water. If the pain is very bad, a swimmer should try to keep his head above water and cry out for help.

If the cramp is not too severe, the swimmer can try to relax by floating on his back. He should then try to contract and relax the stomach muscles while breathing deeply at the same time. Another motion that can help is to bend the knees to the chest, then straighten them again. It may also help to gently knead the stomach muscles with one or both hands.

The best way to avoid a stomach cramp, however, is to stay out of the water for at least an hour after eating a substantial amount of food. This is especially true if you are planning any real strenuous swimming in water over your head. Stomach cramps are nothing to fool with, so this is an important rule of water safety.

Swimmers should also not stay out in the sun for too long. When they come out of the water, they should put on a tee shirt and hat right away, especially if the sun is high in the sky. Too much exposure to the sun's rays can be dangerous.

It is also a good idea for every swimmer to take a course in basic water rescue and lifesaving. The Red Cross offers these courses. You never know when you might have to pull a swimmer in trouble from the water. There are right and wrong ways to do it. Lifesaving techniques today include instruction in CPR (cardiopulmonary resuscitation). The knowledge of CPR is something that could save a life.

Swimming can be both a fun and a competitive sport. But it is a sport in which each participant should be very much aware of the basic rules of safety.

LEARNING HOW TO SWIM

Since this book will concentrate on competitive swimming, it will only go over a few basic points of learning to swim. Once the discussion of the various strokes begins, it is assumed that the participants already know how to swim and do not fear the water.

Step number one for any beginning swimmer, of course, is not to have a fear of the water. If you can't relax in the water, you won't become a confident swimmer. One good way for the begin-

To learn how to swim well, the beginner must feel comfortable with his head under the water. This is necessary for most advanced strokes. One way to get used to this is to stand in waist-deep water, bend over and submerge your face. Get used to exhaling under the water. Turn your face to the side so that your mouth and nose are out of the water, and breathe. Then resubmerge your face. This is the same way you will breathe when swimming the basic crawl.

ner to start is to stand in waist deep water, then bend over and submerge his or her face. A new swimmer must feel comfortable under water. Sometimes this is a difficult thing. Again, it's a matter of relaxation. Someone who can't relax with his face under water will have a tough time becoming a good swimmer and then learning the different strokes.

One good exercise is to submerge only your face from the standing position and exhale under water. Then turn your face to the side, out of the water, and inhale. This is the same type of breathing rhythm used in swimming the basic crawl.

Step number two is to learn to float. Water has a natural buoyancy and will push a body to the surface. Standing in waist deep water, take a deep breath and this time squat down and submerge both head and shoulders. This should be followed by lifting the feet. You will immediately feel yourself beginning to float.

At first, float in a tucked position, legs drawn up. That way, they can be lowered into a standing position at any time. Once a swimmer feels comfortable doing this, he can try a full float. He'll do this by extending his feet behind him and his hands in front of him. By relaxing and floating, he'll quickly feel how the water keeps his body on the surface.

To come out of the full float, just push both arms down very forcefully and at the same time pull both feet down and under the body. It is then easy to resume a standing position. Once the swimmer has confidence in the full float, he may want to try a back float. In this one, the head stays out of the water. Otherwise, it's very similar to the front float.

The swimmer again stands in waist deep water. This time he squats down so the water is just above his shoulders. As he begins to lie back, he extends his legs in front of him and swings his arms out at about a 45 degree angle. If he relaxes, he can lay his head back in the water, but his face will not submerge. The back float can be very relaxing. Once again, the swimmer can return to a standing position by thrusting his arms downward and bringing both legs down and underneath his body.

Learning to float will give a new swimmer more confidence in the water. He should now realize that a relaxed body will not sink. He has also learned to hold his breath and submerge his head in the water. Having done this, he is more than halfway to swimming. All he has to add now is the ability to move his body through the water while using the same principles of relaxing and breathing.

The basic freestyle stroke calls for a *flutter kick*, the movement of the legs up and down under the water. This is easy to practice. One way is to hold onto a stationary object, such as the side of a pool. Grab onto the pool with both hands and extend your body flat out. Then begin to kick up and down with both legs. The correct kick is done with the toes pointed slightly inward. The legs should bend slightly at the knees and only your heels should break the surface of the water. If the entire foot breaks the surface, you're kicking too much.

While holding on to the pool, the swimmer will feel the kicking action forcing his body forward. After practicing this way, he can then take a kickboard and propel himself through the water by holding the board and simply using the flutter kick. A kickboard is made from any buoyant material that will float. It is usually about 10 to 12 inches wide, 18 inches long and two inches thick. The board will hold up the front of the swimmer's body as the kick moves him through the water.

From there, it's just a matter of building the confidence to remove the board and hold up the front of the body by stroking with the hands and arms. Many beginners start with a simple *dog paddle*, in which the hands move in a front-to-back circular motion under the water. Each hand pushes downward and backward,

The beginning swimmer may be reluctant to submerge his head until he has enough confidence. A good way to become comfortable in the water is to swim the dog paddle. Relax, kick your feet up and down, and then move your hands in a circular motion under the water. This will keep you afloat and propel you slowly through the water with your head in the air.

and, with the help of the kick, will move the swimmer through the water. A little more confidence and the arms begin moving in a wider circle. Pretty soon the entire arm and shoulder are being used, and the arms are coming out of the water as they make a wide arc.

When this happens, you are really swimming!

Competitive Swimming

A competitive swimming meet usually takes place in a pool that is 50-meters long. This is called an Olympic-size pool. There are events held using four basic strokes—the *freestyle crawl*, the *backstroke*, the *breaststroke* and the *butterfly*. Each stroke calls for a different technique. Some swimmers prefer to concentrate on just one stroke, while others will try two or even all four.

There are ten individual races and three relay events in an Olympic-style meet. A swimmer joining a team for the first time can choose between shorter and longer races, the different strokes or the relay events. Of course, a good coach will make it easier by being able to tell each swimmer which strokes he feels he will do the best.

Learning The Freestyle Crawl

Most of the basic principles of learning to swim are used in the freestyle crawl. The crawl can be simply a recreational stroke when a person just wants to enjoy a swim. It is also the basic racing stroke used in freestyle swimming. When a swimmer gets into a competitive situation, swimming the crawl correctly becomes all important.

The freestyle crawl uses the flutter kick. It is the same kick the beginning swimmer practiced while holding onto the side of the pool. To repeat, the toes are pointed slightly inward. The knee is not bent to any great degree. The leg action comes from the hip. Each leg should move alternately in an even rhythm. Only the heel of each foot should break the surface of the water.

At the beginning (or entry stage) of the crawl stroke, the swimmer is relaxed. He has extended one arm forward in a line with his shoulder. At this point, the head is submerged, the hand relaxed.

While the kick will help propel the swimmer, most of the speed will come from the arm action. However, the kick helps balance and stabilize the body as it moves through the water. The stronger and faster a swimmer kicks, the faster he will go. He must be careful, however, not to let the kick become a wild, churning motion. It must always be under control, the knee and ankle more relaxed than tensed.

The kicking motion should be no more than 12 inches from the top of the kick to the bottom. A longer kick will sacrifice power and will also throw the swimmer's rhythm off. As a rule, many coaches suggest the swimmer use a six-beat rhythm. This means a total of six kicks (three with each leg) for each stroke with an arm. Some swimmers may find something that works better for them, but the six-beat rhythm is a good way to start bringing leg and arm action together.

Next comes the arm motion. Watch the swimmers at a beach or

Next, the swimmer begins the power part of the stroke, called the thrust. The hand and wrist are now held firm, so the pressure of the water doesn't cause the hand to bend backwards. As the swimmer pulls, he continues to use the flutter kick with both legs.

Midway through the thrust part of the stroke, the opposite arm comes out of the water and loops forward. When the first arm has reached the swimmer's waist, the second arm is entering the water. At this point, the swimmer begins turning his head to breathe.

pool. There will be many different kinds of arm action as they swim. In competition swimming, the technique of the arm action is very important. There is a right way to do it, if you want the best results. Do it any other way and you will lose valuable time during a race, even if you are a naturally powerful swimmer.

Arm action is divided into four distinct stages. These stages are often called by different names. Perhaps the easiest to remember are *entry*, *thrust*, *pull* and *recovery*. Each part of the stroke is repeated over and over again by both arms.

As the swimmer begins his stroke, he extends one arm forward in a direct line with his shoulder. Fingers should be close to each other, but not held together tightly. The palm should be slightly

Many beginning swimmers think their hands should be tightly cupped when swimming the crawl. This is incorrect. The correct way is to keep the fingers relaxed and slightly separated. They should remain relaxed except when the swimmer is pulling through the power part of the stroke.

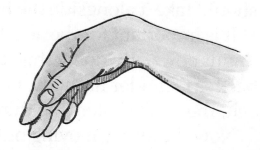

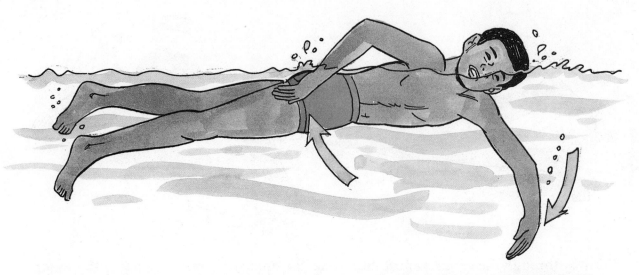

As the second arm begins the thrust part of the stroke, the swimmer turns his head out of the water and takes a quick breath. At this point, the first arm is coming out of the water and is about to loop around for another entry. That part of the stroke is called the recovery. Some swimmers will take a breath on every stroke, others every two strokes.

cupped, the entire hand relaxed, but not limp. In *entry*, the fingertips enter the water first, followed by the entire hand. At this point, the swimmer should begin to feel the pressure of the water against his hand.

Next begins the *thrust*, the power part of the stroke. As the swimmer begins to thrust, the hand, wrist and arm should be in nearly a straight line. The wrist should be held firm enough so that it doesn't begin to bend backward during the stroke. As the swimmer begins to move his arm downward, he also bends it slightly inward so it will pass under his stomach. This surprises some young swimmers who feel the natural course of the arm should take it alongside the body.

It is important for the arm to pass under the stomach for maximum power. By doing this, the swimmer is pushing the water back from under his body. Once the arm passes under the stomach, the stroke enters the third phase, the *pull*.

Now the arm is moving outward, the elbow beginning to

straighten. The swimmer is still putting pressure against the water. When he completes the power part of the stroke, his hand will be back alongside his body. His thumb will be just about touching his thigh. Even though the elbow must bend, then straighten, the stroke must be made in one smooth motion. There should be no jerking of the arm or hitch in the action.

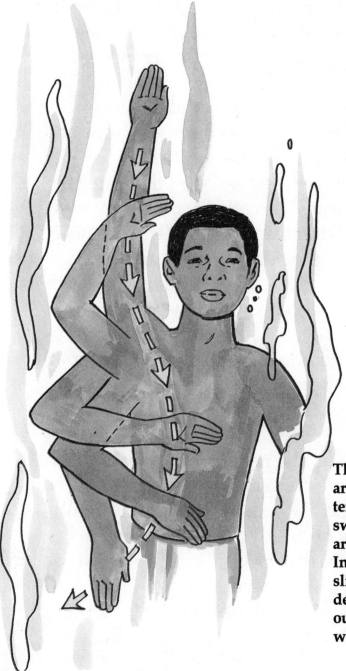

This is the correct path for the arm as it pulls through the water during the crawl stroke. The swimmer does not bring his arm straight down in the water. Instead, the elbow turns out slightly and the arm passes under the swimmer's chest, then outward again to the waist, where the stroke is completed.

29

The final part, *recovery*, is the return of the arm to the beginning position for the next stroke. When the thrust and pull have been completed, the elbow begins to bend once more, and the arm is lifted out of the water. Finally, the forearm and upper arm are nearly at right angles. Then the swimmer reaches his arm forward, straightening his elbow. He is once again ready for entry.

Both the swimmer's arms must work together. It's almost like a windmill action. The arms should always be opposite one another, with the legs keeping up the rhythmic flutter kick. Movement is nonstop as the swimmer cuts through the water. There is no pause from the end of the pull to the beginning of recovery. And no pause from recovery to entry. The complete stroke and kick should be smooth and almost effortless.

There is one other aspect of the freestyle crawl that must be learned. Without the proper way of breathing, a swimmer will tire and run out of gas in the latter stages of the race. Breathing is similar to the exercise in which the beginning swimmer submerged his head and then turned it to the side to take a breath.

The crawl is swum with the head mostly in the water. The swimmer does not raise his head out of the water to breathe. Rather, he turns his head to the side, just enough for his mouth to come out of the water. The swimmer should turn his head to breathe just as the arm on the breathing side begins to come out of the water for the recovery.

Breaths are taken quickly, and the head should return to its downward position by the time the arm is once again in the entry position. The swimmer should also exhale through his mouth and nose just before he turns his head to take a breath. Each swimmer must decide for himself which side he prefers to use for breathing. Whichever side is comfortable is all right.

The crawl is the fastest way a person can swim. Many young teenagers today can swim 50 or 100 meters farther in the same amount of time than the best swimmers of 50 years ago. Learning the correct technique early, then practicing under a good and experienced coach will make you the fastest swimmer you can be.

Learning The Backstroke

The backstroke often follows the crawl when the various strokes are taught to a new swimmer. The reason is that the two strokes are very much alike. In fact, the backstroke has often been called an upside-down crawl. Though it is swum with the swimmer on his back in the water, the arm and leg actions are similar to those in the crawl.

Because the swimmer is on his back, breathing during the backstroke is not really a problem. Once again, the early swimming lessons will come back as an advantage. Anyone wanting to try the backstroke should know how to float on his back. That way, he'll be able to relax more and have the confidence to go ahead and learn the new stroke.

Now it's time to break the backstroke down into its various parts, beginning with the leg kick. As with the crawl, the kick for the backstroke is started by the hips. Like the flutter kick, the backstroke kick is mainly done under the water. Only the toes of the feet may break the surface of the water. Otherwise, the kick will lose some of its effectiveness.

A backstroker must always relax in the water. The stroke begins with the hips near the surface of the water and the head back. When one arm is at the top of the stroke, the other is at the bottom. The arm is straight when it enters the water above the head.

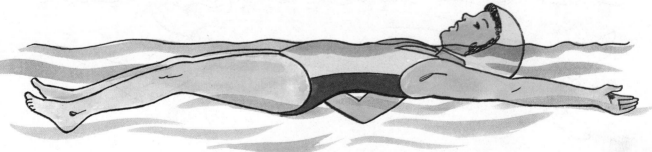

The only difference between the two kicks is in the knee action. The downward action of the feet in the backstroke kick requires a bit more bending at the knees. The feet should be held firm, but relaxed, with the toes pointing outward.

Position of the body for the backstroke is again similar to the floating position. The hips should be held near the surface of the water with the head back, submerged up to the ears. Swimmers should keep their backs slightly arched. This helps keep the hips up and prevents the swimmer from sagging slowly to a sitting position in the water.

Arm action is similar to the crawl in that both arms work opposite each other. In other words, one is at the top of the stroke, while the other is at the bottom. The entry position for the arm is completely straight with no bend in the elbow. It enters the water at a point just past the straight-out extension from the shoulder.

The hands are almost at a right angle to the water, tilted just slightly toward the water, with the palms facing away from the body. The hands will drop some four to six inches into the water

As the swimmer strokes, a flutter kick is used, similar to the crawl. The swimmer's upper arm is submerged four to six inches under the water before she begins to pull, using her hand almost like an oar. Halfway through the stroke, the motion changes from pulling to pushing.

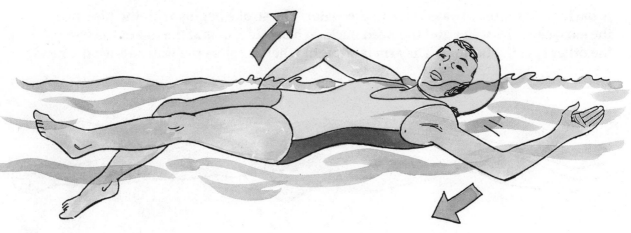

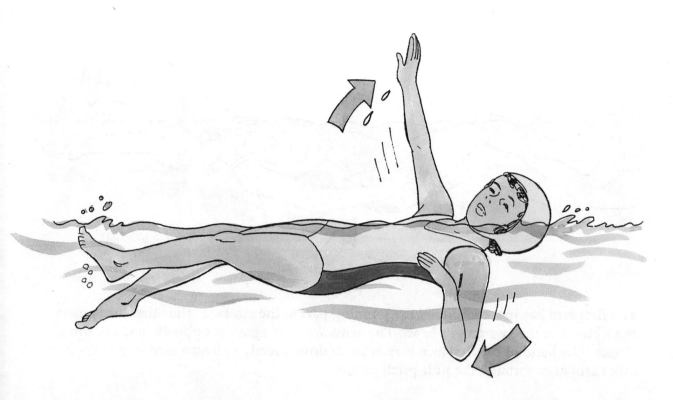

As the first arm is halfway through the stroke and ready to begin pushing the water, the second arm is out of the water in the recovery phase. The feet continue to flutter kick for the entire stroke.

before beginning the pulling part of the stroke. As the arm begins pulling forward, the hand and inside of the arm push the water backward and toward the feet.

At the lowest point of the stroke, the arm might be eight or nine inches below the surface. Then it moves parallel to the surface, continuing to push the water toward the feet. At the completion of the stroke, the arm is again close to the thigh, with the palm of the hand facing the surface of the water.

Now the arm is ready for recovery. It is lifted straight out of the water and brought straight up in a windmill motion. At the highest point, the swimmer should be sure to once again turn the palm outward so he is ready for the next entry. As with the crawl, the kick and arm action should be coordinated with a six-beat stroke rhythm.

The first arm has just completed the pushing part of the stroke as the other arm enters the water over the swimmer's head. The arms are once again at opposite ends of the stroke. The hand of the first arm is now palm down, ready to begin recovery as the other arm goes through the pull-push phase.

The swimmer must also be certain to keep his arms working smoothly and exactly opposite each other. As one hand completes its push of the water and is alongside the thigh, the other arm must once again be entering the water to continue the motion. While the swimmer's head is not submerged, breathing should be done in a smooth and regular pattern.

One rule is to inhale as the right hand comes out of the water, then to exhale as the left hand comes out. This will take practice. But because the body is more buoyant with air in the lungs, this regular pattern of breathing will also help keep the swimmer high in the water. Doing it this way will give the overall stroke a smoother and more rhythmic motion, the kind it takes to swim your best time and to possibly win the race.

Of course, the best way to judge if you are stroking correctly is to be watched by a good coach. You can also practice your strokes on dry land just to get an idea of the motion. This can easily be done for both the crawl and backstroke by lying on a narrow bench. Your arms will be able to extend both above and below your body, and you can simulate the stroke with great accuracy.

As with all competitive swimming strokes, the better your technique, the better your times. Also, a good coach and hours of quality practice time will allow you to become better and better as you work toward a winning goal.

Learning The Breaststroke

There is nothing new about the breaststroke. In fact, it is one of the oldest ways of swimming and in some places is still looked upon as a beginner's stroke. Some people even think humans learned the breaststroke by watching frogs swim through the water. The leg kick in the breaststroke looks like the leg kick of a frog and is actually called a *frog kick*.

The breaststroke is the slowest of the four racing strokes. It is also the only one of the four in which both the arms and legs remain underwater during the entire movement. Unlike the other strokes, the use of the legs in the breaststroke is as important as the arms in helping the swimmer reach maximum speed.

In the starting position for the breaststroke, the head is submerged and the hands are just under the chin, thumbs almost touching. The swimmer will then thrust both arms forward just before starting the power part of the stroke.

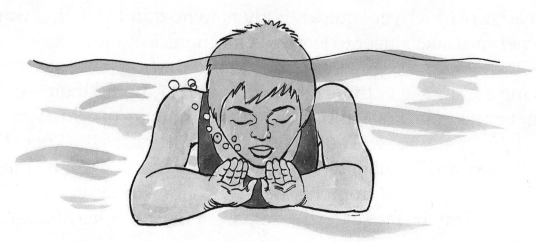

As the swimmer begins to pull with both arms, the body is at its highest point in the water. The swimmer will take a breath about halfway through the arm stroke.

Like other strokes, the breaststroke can be broken down into three separate movements involving the arms, legs and head. None should be particularly difficult to learn. But putting all three together is sometimes more difficult than it appears.

The first step in learning the stroke is to master the kick. It is very different from the flutter kick used in both the crawl and the backstroke. Some young swimmers seem to have a natural frog type of kick when they first learn to swim. They can pick up the breaststroke kick very quickly. Others, who don't kick that way, sometimes take longer to learn the mechanics of the kick.

One way for a beginner to understand the frog kick is to stand facing a wall, two or three inches distant. He should then raise his leg, bending the knee until his shin and thigh form a 90 degree, or right, angle. He will quickly find that if he raises the knee directly forward, it will hit the wall. To bring the knee up, he must also turn it outward from the wall. When the knee is up, he should move the leg so the inside part of the knee, leg and ankle are just touching the wall. This is almost the exact position of the legs at the start of the frog kick.

This exercise can also be done while standing in the shallow end of the pool, facing the wall. Once the swimmer has a good idea of the basic movement, he can try it by hanging onto the side of the pool and extending his body flat in the water.

The swimmer's legs will actually begin the kick from about a six-inch depth in the water. Next the knees will be drawn up toward the body. The swimmer then draws his legs apart, the feet and ankles outside the knees, toes pointing downward and outward. The movement is then completed by thrusting the soles of the feet against the water, straightening the legs and at the same time snapping them back together.

If the kick is done correctly, the swimmer will feel the pressure as the water is pushed by the inside of the foot, leg and thigh, all working together. Even if the swimmer is holding the end of the pool, a correct kick will give him or her the feeling of being forced forward and upward.

The next step in mastering the frog kick is to practice it by hold-

The stroke itself is short and powerful. It ends when the arms are even with the shoulders. At that point, the swimmer will begin the recovery phase.

During the recovery stage of the breaststroke, the swimmer begins to bring her arms together so they will again meet under her chin. At this point, the swimmer exhales under water.

ing a kickboard. This will keep the front end of the swimmer's body afloat and allow him to feel the force of the kick and how it will propel him through the water. Once a beginner can use the frog kick correctly, it's time to begin putting it together with the arm movement of the stroke. Arm movement begins with the arms reaching straight forward in front of the swimmer. Like the legs, the arms should be about six inches below the surface of the water. The swimmer should turn his wrists inward and bring his hands together so that the index fingers of both hands are touching each other.

The stroke itself is a short, hard outward pull. It is not a long arc. The arm action is stopped at a point where the hands are just about in line with the shoulders. At this point, the elbows are bent inward and the hands brought back to a position just under the chin. They are then thrust forward so the stroke can begin again. It is a power stroke that must be very forceful. The short-

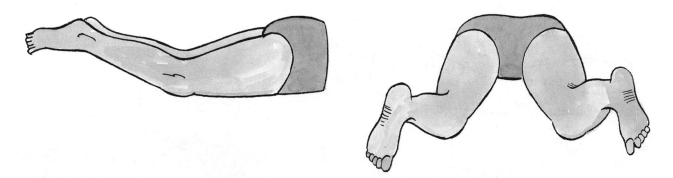

It is important for every breaststroker to know how to do the frog kick. Both leg and arm movements must work together. The swimmer begins with legs relaxed and straight back. He then separates his knees and begins to draw his feet up toward his buttocks, as shown here.

ness of the stroke adds to the power. A long, lazy stroke might be relaxing for recreational swimming, but not for a competitive breaststroker.

Now it's time to bring the leg and arm movements together. The breaststroke is the only stroke in which the arms and legs stroke alternately. Thus the body is moving forward at all times, first pulled by the arms, then pushed by the legs. The following tips should help any swimmer coordinate his movements.

At the same time the arms pull hard, the legs are drawn up into

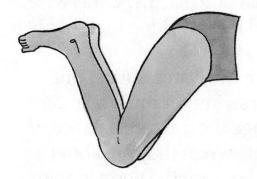

When the feet are drawn up, the heels are almost touching. But the knees are still held apart. Next, the swimmer will turn his feet downward and then straighten his legs.

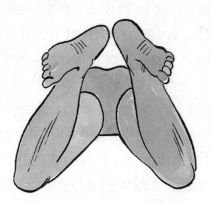

39

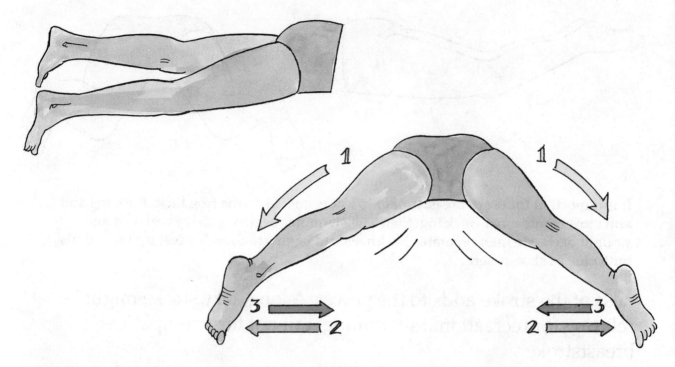

The legs are straightened away from the body. They are now in a position to drive inward, propelling the swimmer forward. The arm pull and the leg snap are done opposite one another. That way, the swimmer is moving forward at all times. There is a very brief glide between the leg snap and the next thrust of the arms.

the ready position. Then, as the arms move around and come forward again, the legs complete the frog kick. There is a brief glide between the leg snap and the next thrust of the arms. Otherwise, the stroke is continuous, with arms and legs working together in a smooth rhythm.

Even though the head is mostly out of the water during this stroke, breathing is still important. The swimmer must take care not to breathe in a way that might change the delicate balance of the body. As a rule, breaststrokers inhale when they are about halfway through their arm pull. That's because the body is at its highest point in the water during this phase of the stroke.

The swimmer will then exhale as the arms are under the body beginning their recovery and the head is again lower in the water. Breathing should always be smooth and controlled. Sometimes a breaststroker will exhale while his mouth and nose are just under the surface of the water. This is up to the individual. As long as the basic rules of breathing are observed, a slight difference in head position should not affect the results.

Breaststrokers may not go as fast as swimmers in other events. But most of them take great pride in mastering the stroke and becoming good at it. Since nearly everyone swims some sort of breast stroke while in the water, the competitive version of the stroke should be something every swimmer wants to try.

Learning The Butterfly

The butterfly is strictly a competitive swimming stroke. You won't see too many people swimming the butterfly for fun at the beach or in a pool. The stroke is very different from the others and requires strength, rhythm and coordination. A good butterfly swimmer will know he has really accomplished something after he has mastered the stroke.

People often compare the movements in the butterfly to the

In the butterfly stroke, both arms work together. During the recovery part of the stroke, they both loop out of the water from back to front, entering again in front of the swimmer, as shown. The swimmer also uses a dolphin kick, with both legs moving up and down in unison. The leg kick comes all the way from the hips, giving the whole body the up and down movement of a dolphin.

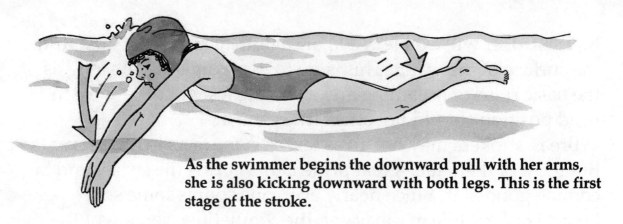

As the swimmer begins the downward pull with her arms, she is also kicking downward with both legs. This is the first stage of the stroke.

movements of a dolphin. The butterfly swimmer moves in a smooth up and down, wavelike motion. In fact, the kick used to swim the butterfly is called a *dolphin kick*. The arm movements are also different—that is, the recovery part of the stroke takes place with the arms out of the water.

This may sound quite complicated at first. For that reason, it isn't a bad idea for young swimmers to watch a good butterfly swimmer in action before beginning to learn the stroke.

With the butterfly, leg action must be coordinated with the movement of the entire body. It is good overall body rhythm that makes the kick effective. If the swimmer does it right, he can move through the water without even using his arms.

In some ways, the dolphin kick is similar to the flutter kick. Both kicks begin at the hip and require only a slight bend of the knee. The difference is that with the dolphin kick, both feet stroke at the same time. In other words, the feet move together, not opposite one another, as they do with the flutter kick.

A beginning butterfly swimmer will first have to learn the correct body position for swimming the stroke. A good way to practice this is to lie in the water, face down, in a floating position. The swimmer should place his arms at his side, take a deep breath and then drop his head under the surface.

As he drops his head, he should also drop his shoulders lower in the water. He will notice immediately that his hips are forced to

42

move upward. As the hips come up, the head is lifted and the hips will be forced back down. When a short, but strong downward kick is added with both feet, the swimmer has found the basic movement for the butterfly.

When the hips move upward, the swimmer will bend both legs slightly at the knee. The heels come close to the surface of the water. The toes are pointed and may break the surface slightly. Then, as the head comes up and the hips start downward, the swimmer straightens his legs as he kicks downward with both feet. This is the lower-body movement of the butterfly stroke. Now it's time to add the arm movement.

Again, arm movement in the butterfly is different than all other strokes. The entry point is out in front of the swimmer, arms straight, hands about a shoulder width apart. The hands then start down and slightly to the side, catching the water. With the elbows kept up, the swimmer then pulls his arms downward toward his hips. A final hard push leaves the arms extended backward, by the swimmer's side.

The force of the arms pushing down also forces the body toward the surface. When her arms are at their lowest point, the swimmer raises her head and takes a breath. She also brings her legs back up toward the surface. Only the heels of the feet should break the surface of the water.

As the arms complete the pull, the head goes back into the water and the legs once again kick downward. The swimmer's elbows have already broken water. They will be followed by the arms as they loop out of the water to begin the next stroke.

The recovery, which is unique to the butterfly, is made by bringing the arms upward and out of the water. They are then swung in a wide arc past the swimmer's head and wind up outstretched in front of the swimmer for another entry.

Perhaps the toughest part of swimming the butterfly is the co-ordination of arms, legs and breathing. The swimmer will inhale when his arms are at the deepest point of the stroke. The arms help push the head up so he can gulp a breath of air. He then plunges his head back into the water for the completion of the stroke and the recovery. He will exhale under the water as the arms come out of the water to begin the recovery. Some butterfly swimmers will breathe on every stroke. Others breathe every two strokes. It is up to the individual swimmer to decide which method of breathing is right for him.

The first downward leg kick comes as the swimmer begins the pulling stage of the stroke. As he completes the stroke and breathes, the legs once again start up. A second downward kick occurs as the swimmer completes the stroke, just before he starts his recovery. Then the legs come up again during recovery, ready to kick downward at the start of the next stroke.

Getting everything to work together is the most difficult part of swimming the butterfly. It takes a good coach to work with you, for the butterfly is a challenging stroke. Those who become good at it can be proud. They really have achieved something in the sport of swimming.

The Racing Dive

Like a sprinter ready to burst out of the starting blocks, a good swimmer must be able to get a strong start. How he enters the water can mean the difference between winning and losing. Except for the backstroke, which starts with the swimmers already in the water, the other three strokes all begin with the competitors diving into the pool from a starting platform. It is an absolute must for each competitor to know the basic racing dive.

The racing dive is made from a raised platform at the end of the pool. For this reason, it is important for every swimmer to know the basic principles of diving. He must also be confident enough to make a simple dive off the end of the pool before trying the racing dive off the platform.

Perhaps the first thing to remember when learning to dive is that if the head dives right, the rest of the body will follow. It is essential to hold the head in the correct way when making any kind of dive. To learn this, simply start by sitting at the edge of a pool with your feet on the first underwater rung of the ladder. Do this in at least five feet of water, however. In fact, every swimmer must know that he should NEVER dive into shallow water, and NEVER dive into water where the depth is unknown. To do so is to invite a head or neck injury, or worse.

Sitting on the ladder in the deep end of the pool, the beginning diver should then tuck his head down until his chin is resting on his chest. Then he should put his arms out in front of him so they are pointing into the water. Keeping the head down, he should

Three of the four racing strokes described thus far begin with the swimmer diving into the water. Therefore, every competitive swimmer must know how to make a racing dive. Once on the platform, the swimmer should spread his feet shoulder-width apart, the toes curled over the end of the platform. He should bend forward at the waist and also bend the knees slightly. His arms should be out in front of his body and his eyes focused on a spot in the water.

then roll forward into the water. The important thing is to keep the head down until he feels himself heading toward the bottom.

At this point, the diver can arch his back and tilt his hands upward. By tilting the hands and lifting the head, he will start back up to the surface. Once this is done with the head staying down, then the beginner can begin to dive from a standing position. First he should try it from the step on the ladder. Then from the edge of the pool. Once he has confidence, it is time to dive from a board or from the starting platform.

The key is confidence and keeping the head down. Always remember to never let your head come untucked until you are in the water. That way, there is little chance for a belly flop or badly mistimed dive.

Now on to the racing dive. Once again, the technique can be practiced from the edge of the pool first. Begin with the feet spread to shoulder width and the toes curled over the edge of the pool. On the platform, you would assume this position at the command, "Swimmers up!"

When the gun sounds, the swimmer must move quickly. He begins by swinging his arms back. He is also up on his toes. He will spring with his legs and push off with his toes at the same time he throws his arms forward. A strong forward motion of the arms will help him leap out over the water.

The next command would be, "Take your mark!" That's when the swimmers assume the starting position. This is done by bending forward at the waist, with just a slight bend of the knees. The eyes should be focused both downward at the water and forward. The arms straighten and are held out in front of the body, hands pointing toward the water.

When the gun sounds, the swimmers spring into action. The arms swing back, then forward, in a strong motion to help propel the body out over the water. At the same time, the legs spring forward as if the swimmer is making a standing broad jump. He uses the edge of the pool or the starting platform to push off.

In a split second, the swimmer's entire body is stretched out over the water. Even though the swimmer is leaping over the water, the movement of the head and shoulders should be downward. The head, as always, should be tucked tight to the chest.

As the swimmer leaps out over the water, his entire body should be stretched out. It is important to remember that the head and shoulders should always be moving downward. The head should also remain tucked tight to the chest. A smooth entry into the water is very important. That gives the swimmer more glide and forward momentum as he starts his stroke.

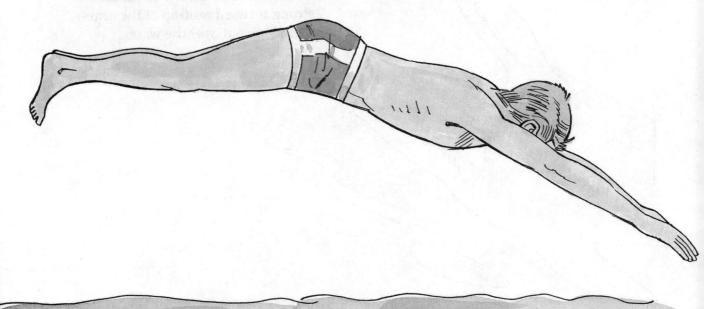

It is important for a swimmer to leap as far out over the water as he can. but he must also make sure his body makes a smooth entry into the pool. A smooth entry will give him more forward momentum, and it will also make it easier for him to begin his stroke as soon as he hits the water.

Once the technique of the dive has been mastered, the swimmer can move from the edge of the pool to the starting platform. From there it's just a matter of practice. A swimmer must concentrate hard on his start. He must be alert, quick and have fast reactions. All of these qualities produce a better dive, a better start and a better chance to win.

The Backstroke Start

The backstroke begins with the swimmers in the water. They hold onto a rail that is attached to the end of the starting platform. The toes are placed on the wall of the pool right about at the water level. When the command, ''Take your mark!'' is given, the back-

The backstroke is the only event in which the swimmers start while in the water. There is a rail on the front of the starting platform that the swimmer holds with both hands. He then places his toes on the wall near the water line. Just before the start, he should pull himself into a tight, tucked ball against the pool wall and the starting platform.

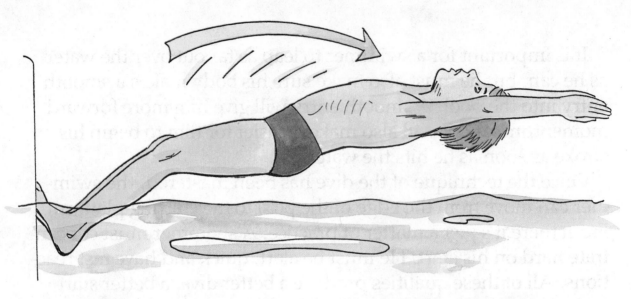

At the sound of the gun, the swimmer must move quickly. He pulls hard on the starting bar with his arms, lifting himself further out of the water. As he is doing this, he pushes hard with his legs, throwing his body away from the wall and out over the water. Next, he should throw his head back and stretch his arms overhead as far as they will go. Arching the back will help the swimmer extend his body over the water. Then, as he hits the water, he should tuck his chin and pull one arm through the stroke to get him back to the surface of the water. He then begins to stroke with both arms and kick with the legs. The race is on.

stroker pulls himself into a tight, tucked ball against the wall and starting platform.

When the gun sounds, the swimmer lifts himself upward with a strong pull of the arms. At the same time, he pushes himself away from the wall with a powerful thrust of the legs. He then throws the head back and stretches the arms over his head. A strong push will bring most of his body out and over the water.

At this point, he should arch his back, extending his body as far as he can. When he hits the water, he should immediately tuck his chin and use one backstroke arm pull to return to the surface as quickly as possible. From there, it's into the stroke and the race.

Though the backstroke start is different from the racing dive, both starts are extremely important to a successful race. They should be practiced under the watchful eye of a good coach. Without a good start, it will be a lot more difficult to win.

50

Learning How To Turn

In any race longer than one length of the pool, the swimmer is going to have to turn around and come back. Unless a swimmer knows the proper way to turn, he will lose valuable seconds each time he comes to the wall. A smooth, quick turn can be the difference between winning and losing.

There is no one way to turn at the end of a lap. In fact, the different strokes dictate different types of turns. With some strokes, there are several turns to choose from, some more difficult than others.

Let's start with the freestyle crawl. With the crawl, there are two different turns a swimmer can use. The first is called the *freestyle open turn*. Remember, the only requirement for a legal turn is that some part of the body touch the wall. All swimmers must also make sure that they are not concentrating so much on their swimming that they lose track of just where the wall is.

With the open turn, the swimmer reaches out with one arm as he nears the wall. The head and body follow the outstretched arm to the wall and begin to turn in the direction of the arm. At the

For many years, swimmers have used the freestyle open turn when swimming the crawl. The swimmer begins by reaching for the wall with one arm. At the same time, she should begin to lean slightly to the side of the outstretched arm.

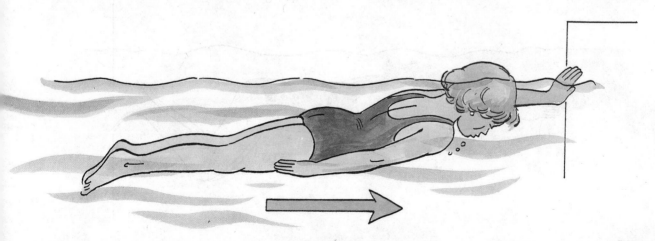

Next the swimmer pulls herself into a tucked position near the wall, using her free arm to help maneuver her body. She also begins the turn as she goes into her tuck. It is important to remember to bring both feet in together, so they are in a position to make contact with the wall.

same time, the other arm begins to hook the water, directing the body into a tucked position alongside the wall.

Once tucked close to the wall, the body then rotates in the direction of the free arm. The last part of the spin is made basically

The final part of the turn is made with the feet touching the wall. As the swimmer completes the turn, her head can break the water, enabling her to take a quick breath. But she should quickly submerge her head as she pushes her body away from the wall. A strong thrust with the legs off the pool wall gives the swimmer the momentum to resume the stroke.

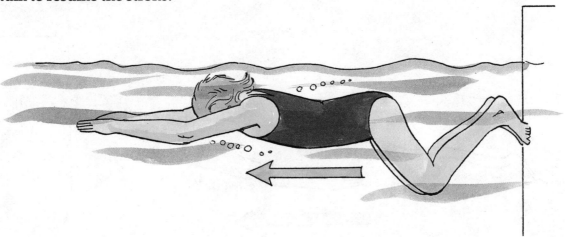

with the feet, both of which are now touching the wall. Then the head and the free arm begin leading the rest of the body away from the wall. At this point, the swimmer's head breaks the surface of the water for the first time since the turn began. This enables the swimmer to take a breath.

After the quick breath, the swimmer points his turning arm and free arm away from the wall, and then puts his head back underwater between both arms. He is now ready to push off. The push is made with a strong thrust from both legs. At the same time, the swimmer again extends his body all the way out. This helps to get the maximum glide at a slight upward angle, so he will again emerge at the surface.

As soon as the swimmer feels the glide is beginning to slow, he quickly resumes his flutter kick and begins the crawl stroke.

The second freestyle turn has become very popular in recent years because swimmers who do it well feel they can turn faster. It is called the *tumble*, or *flip turn*, and it is exactly the way it sounds. As the swimmer approaches the wall, he tucks his head

Today, many freestyle swimmers prefer the tumble, or flip turn, in which neither arm touches the end of the pool. As the swimmer nears the wall, he tucks his head and body into a ball. Then, using his arms to guide him, he does a complete tumble, or flip, in the water.

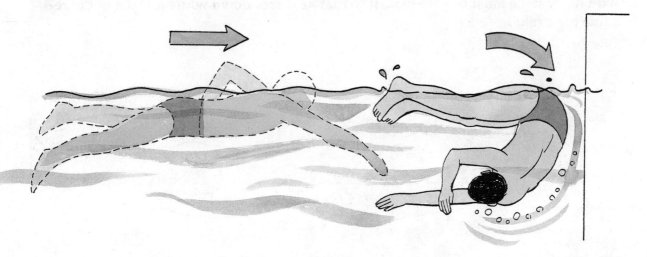

Timing is very important with the flip turn because the swimmer must be close enough to the wall to get a good push off with his feet. If he is too close, he may hit the wall when starting his flip and lose precious time.

and body into a tight ball. With a thrust of his arms, he does a forward flip, or tumble, in the water.

Timing is all important with the flip turn. The swimmer must make sure his body doesn't hit the wall, but he must be close enough so that both legs can contact the wall and give him a strong push in the opposite direction. With the flip turn, the hands never touch the wall.

The tricky part of the turn is twisting the body while pushing off. When the swimmer's feet contact the wall, his body is sometimes sideways in the water. As he thrusts with his feet, he must be sure to turn so that he is face down while gliding out to resume his stroke.

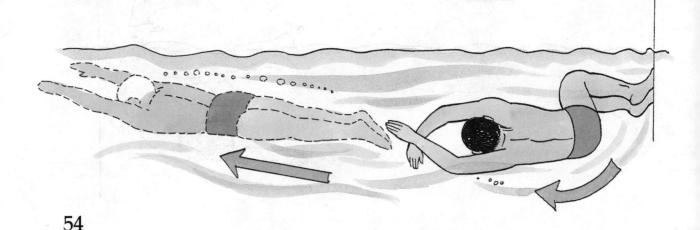

The tricky part of the flip turn is twisting the body so that when the swimmer pushes off, he is once again gliding face down. He wants to come out of the turn the same way a swimmer using the open turn would. The twist is accomplished by hooking the water with the arms and then completing the twist with the feet when they contact the wall.

A freestyle swimmer may want to learn both methods of turning. Most swimmers today use the flip turn because they can reverse direction very fast. Let your coach advise you on the best thing for your age and skill level.

Those swimming the backstroke will have their own special turn to learn. The rules say that backstrokers must stay on their backs until they touch the wall and begin their turn. Therefore, the swimmer cannot make a turning move until his hand hits the end of the pool. While the swimmer may roll to the side while turning, when he pushes off, he must be on his back once again.

The backstroker will turn in the direction of the hand that touches the wall. A swimmer who prefers to turn right will have to make sure that his right hand hits the wall first. Those who prefer to turn left must hit the wall with their left hands.

Backstrokers must remain on their backs until they make contact with the wall. The swimmer here has made contact with the palm of her hand and is already beginning the backstroke flip turn.

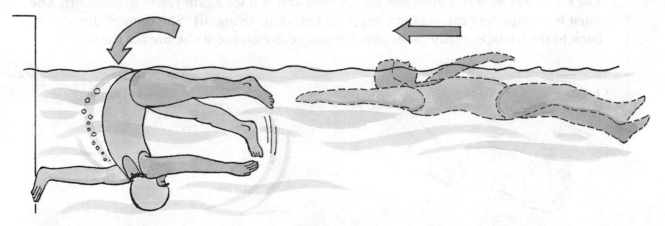

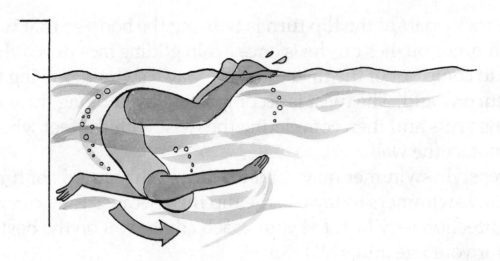

As she goes into the full turn, the backstroker tucks her body in close to the wall, so she will be able to push off with both feet. She uses her arms to help complete the flip.

Most swimmers will touch with the palm of the hand flat against the wall, thumb up. As soon as the touch is made, the swimmer begins to roll in the direction of the turn. He also bends the elbow of the touching arm, bringing his body in closer to the wall. When the knees are tucked together tight to the chest, he spins his body to the right toward the wall. The left arm pushes back against the water to help with the turn.

The swimmer keeps turning until his back is to the open end of the pool and both feet are on the wall, just a few inches below the

The swimmer now has both feet on the wall and is once again ready to push off. She must be completely turned onto her back before pushing off. She then glides slowly back to the surface, ready to resume her stroke the moment she breaks the water.

surface of the water. The swimmer's body is still drawn up with knees against the chest, and now the hands join the feet on the wall. The head is just above the surface, and the swimmer can take a quick breath.

Once the swimmer has taken his breath, he lowers his hips, and his head and shoulders once again submerge in the water. The hands are now brought off the wall and with fingers leading, are swung carefully past the shoulders. They will wind up reaching overhead but should not break the surface of the water.

The swimmer then pushes hard off the wall with both feet, arms fully extended and body gliding at a slight angle toward the surface. The legs begin kicking almost immediately, and as soon as the head breaks the surface at the end of the glide, the swimmer resumes stroking with both arms. He has completed the backstroke turn.

Turns for both the butterfly and breaststroke are identical. In each stroke, the swimmer must touch the wall with both hands at the same level and at the same time. As with the backstroke, the turn can be made to either side.

As the swimmer approaches the wall, he reaches out with both hands, grabbing the wall. He then bends both elbows slightly and brings his head and tucked body in to the wall. At this point, head and shoulders are well above the surface of the water. The swimmer turns in whichever direction feels more comfortable.

The head turns to lead the body around. At the same time, both arms push off the wall and extend to the side to help speed up the turn. The swimmer takes a breath as the hand on the turning side begins reaching out ahead of the swimmer. The other hand comes off and is alongside the head. At this point, the swimmer has no contact with the wall.

As the head drops into the water between the arms, the second arm extends outward and the swimmer completes the turn. The legs then reach out so both feet can contact the wall. The swimmer should be close enough so that his knees are still well bent when contact is made. That way they will get a strong push.

At this point, the butterfly or breaststroke swimmer is in an identical position as the freestyler coming off the open or flip turn. A strong push and glide put the swimmer in position to resume his regular stroke.

Turns are as important as the stroke itself. Depending on the length of a race, a swimmer is going to make one or more turns. Even the fastest swimmer will find it difficult to win if he loses valuable time on each turn. Turns are well worth working on, perfecting and practicing.

A Word About Distance Swimming

There are some swimmers who may not find the standard competitive races to their liking. They may love to swim, but want to compete in other ways. Like the runner who likes to run marathons, a swimmer may decide he gets more pleasure out of very long swims. This is a very healthful and challenging approach to the sport.

Like slow, long distance jogging, distance swimming is very good for both body and mind. But anyone who wants to swim longer distances should know the variations in the basic stroke.

It doesn't matter if the swimmer is just doing many laps in a pool or is swimming in a lake or river. If he is going to swim a long distance, he must always remember to relax. This means creating as little muscle tension as possible. As muscles get tired from repeated use, there is sometimes a tendency for them to cramp. One way to relax the arm muscles is to be sure to use the *bent-arm recovery*. The distance swimmer will use the basic crawl stroke of freestyle racers. But he is not looking for every ounce of speed and power he can get. The bent-arm recovery is one way to get that needed rest for the muscles.

Instead of swinging the arm high during the recovery phase of the stroke, the swimmer will simply bend his elbow high enough to get his hand and forearm out of the water. He then moves his hand in a straight line just over the surface of the water to the forward entry position.

This is a smooth, fast recovery, but it allows the forearm to relax as it moves forward, because it is the shoulder movement that flops it forward. The brief second of relaxation helps the muscles to recover before the next stroke.

Another good thing about the bent-arm recovery is that it allows both of the swimmer's arms to be pulling at once, if only for a split second. One is pulling at the beginning of its power stroke, while the other is still pulling at the end of the stroke. It takes a great deal of practice to get the timing of the stroke just right. Both hands are pulling at once, even only for a brief instant, helping to propel the swimmer, and taking some of the pressure off the arms.

The key to distance swimming is smoothness. The less motion the better. Most coaches recommend six kicks for each full stroke of one arm. As with the shorter distances, the kicking motion must be in rhythm with the arm strokes. It should not change with each stroke.

Breathing is very important in long distance swimming. Proper breathing will keep the swimmer from getting tired too quickly. The breathing method is the same as for the freestyle crawl. It is very important to keep a good, steady flow of oxygen in the system. To do this, the distance swimmer must be sure to take a full, deep breath each time and to also exhale fully. Then the oxygen exchange will be complete with each stroke.

Distance swimming is just another aspect of one of the most popular sports in the world. Everyone should know how to swim. It is a fun and healthful sport, but it is also a skill that any of us may need suddenly at any time. Over the years, many people have been saved from drowning because the first person on the scene knew how to swim and what to do.

To be a championship swimmer takes many hours of practice. Whether you swim one stroke or several, you've got to work hard to be the best you can be. Then, when you're part of a team, you can make that practice pay and have that special feeling of being number one.

Also, many people have saved their own lives because they knew how to swim. They used the skill to reach land or stay afloat long enough to be rescued. But these, of course, are extreme examples. The fun and healthy part should come first.

As mentioned at the beginning of the book, anyone can learn to swim. The only basic requirements are to have no fear of the water and to relax. Then find someone who has patience and knows how to teach. It won't take long before you're floating, then doing the dog paddle and finally swimming.

After that, you can decide if you want to pursue the sport competitively. If you do, you'll have several different strokes and several distances to choose from. A good coach can teach you each one. Once you learn them, you'll be able enjoy swimming even more than ever. Who knows, someday you, too, may be able to compete in the Olympic Games.

Glossary

Backstroke A recreational and competitive stroke in which the swimmer lies on his back in the water and strokes with one arm at a time. The head is out of the water and the swimmer is moving backwards.

Backstroke turn The way in which a backstroker must turn during a race. The swimmer must touch the edge of the pool with one hand, can roll over in either direction, but must be on his back again when he pushes off.

Breaststroke A recreational and racing stroke in which both arms and legs remain underwater during the entire cycle of the stroke.

Breathing The various ways a competitive swimmer must breathe with each individual stroke. Correct breathing is an important part of successful racing.

Butterfly Perhaps the most difficult of the racing strokes. Both arms and legs must work together, and breathing is very important. The butterfly has been described as imitating the movements of a dolphin.

Butterfly and breaststroke turn Identical turns in which the swimmer must touch the side of the pool with both hands at the same level at the same time.

Cramp A sudden, painful contraction or tightening of the muscles. Leg and foot cramps can come from fatigue. Dangerous stomach cramps usually come from swimming too soon after eating.

Crawl The fastest of all the strokes and the most popular in both recreational and competitive swimming. The crawl is swum with the body flat in the water, face down, and uses a combination of arm and leg strength.

Distance swimming Any swim longer than 1,500 meters. It can be anything from recreational swimming that resembles jogging to a long, challenging swim across the English Channel.

Diving A means of entering the water in which the arms and head are the first points of entry.

Dog paddle An elementary swimming stroke often used by beginning swimmers. The hands are kept below the surface of the water and move in a circular motion, much like the way a dog swims.

Dolphin kick The required kick of butterfly swimmers. Both legs and feet are held together and must move in unison.

Entry Term used to describe the way a diver or swimmer enters the water. It is also the point at which the arm and hand enter the water during some racing strokes.

Float The act of relaxing and being held up by the natural buoyancy of the water. It's a sign of confidence in the water when a beginning swimmer learns to float.

Flutter kick A rapid up and down movement of the legs under water used in several swimming strokes. The legs and feet always move in opposite directions from one another.

Freestyle A term that means a swimmer can use any technique he wishes during a race. But today all freestyle swimmers use the basic crawl stroke.

Freestyle flip turn A popular turn in which the swimmer does a forward roll, or somersault, after touching the end of the pool. Most top racers use this style of turn today.

Freestyle open turn The more traditional method of turning in which the swimmer turns in one direction or the other after touching the end of the pool.

Frog kick A style of kick used in swimming the breaststroke. The legs move up and out, then snap together, much like the legs of a frog.

Kickboard A board or support made of a buoyant material. A young swimmer can hold on to the board with his hands while practicing his kick and get the feel of moving through the water.

Lap Term used to describe one length of a swimming pool. If the swimmer goes back and forth, he has swum two laps.

Racing dive The way swimmers enter the water for all races, except the backstroke. The dive is made from a raised platform at the edge of the pool. If done correctly, it can give a swimmer an early advantage.

Recovery Term given to the part of the stroke in which the arm and hand return to begin the stroke once again. In most cases, the arm comes out of the water during recovery.

Stroke A particular way of swimming, depending on how the arms and legs are used. Each stroke has certain movements that must be followed to make it legal in competition.

Turn The way in which a swimmer changes direction when he has reached one end of the pool and must start back the other way.